The First Steps of Martial Arts for Kids

I CAN LEARN KARATE

DAVID NEMEROFF

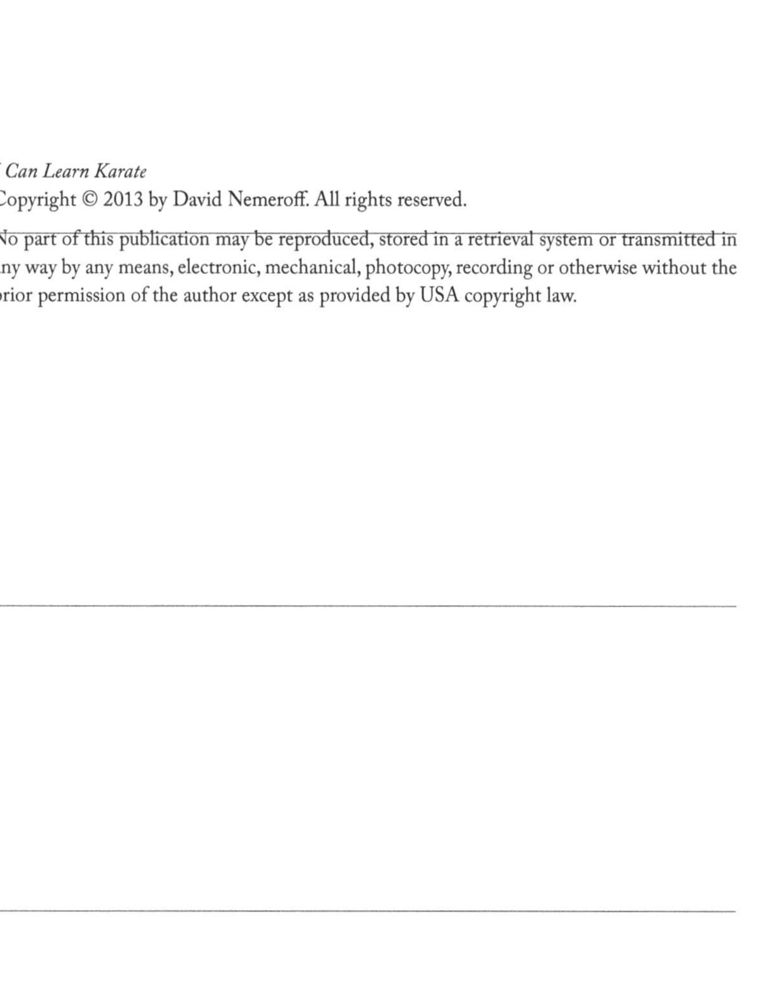

DEDICATION

This book is dedicated to my son, Elijah. You bring such joy to my life. I hope to share all of my knowledge, passion and experience with you in the years to come. This book is written for you and other children who I hope will benefit as much from the martial arts as I have.

ACKNOWLEDGEMENTS

I would like to thank everyone who participated in the creation of this book including students Michaela Steele, Liam Zarrizski, Michael Weber Jr., Jaivon Morgan, Grayson Galligani and Paulette Guzy, who modeled for this book. Additionally, I would like to show my gratitude to Jessica Galligani for all of her help and expertise taking the photos.

There are many great things
at a martial arts school,
A lot you can learn,
which are all very cool.
You can put on a uniform,
known as a gi,

Then tie your rank belt, called an obi.

David Nemeroff

You can learn how to stand.

You can learn how to bow.
It is great for respect. I can show you how.

I can throw a fast punch
really quick in the air.

Then I hit all the pads
over here, over there.

I can snap out a kick
with the flick of my leg.
I can show you much more
and there's no need to beg.

I can stand on one foot,
balance on a tall stool.
It is all for defense.
That's a key golden rule.

I can get in a stance.

I can do a fun throw.

There is so much to see,
like a rising elbow.

You can train how to grapple or escape from a lock,

David Nemeroff

Tie a foe like a pretzel,

or defend with a block.

Learn to fall and roll over long wooden sticks.

Gain the focus you need to break through solid bricks.

Now that we've shown a few
moves you can learn,
I will repeat them then
you take a turn.

Hit a pad,   grapple,   balance,

stance,   kick.

Punch,   roll, fall,

throw,   you better block quick.

Bow to the teacher to show her respect,
And that is a lesson you shouldn't neglect.

There are many fun things that are taught for defense.
It is great what you'll learn, plus you'll build confidence.

Now, let's practice a few
moves together!

Front Punch

To begin a front punch, stand with your feet shoulder width apart and fists up.

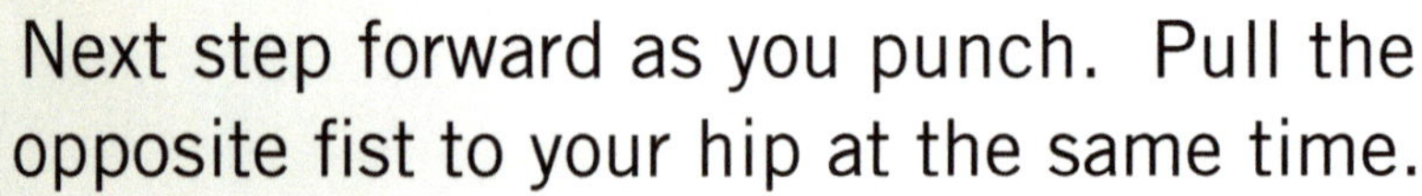

Next step forward as you punch. Pull the opposite fist to your hip at the same time.

Front Kick

To begin a front kick, stand in a ready stance with your hands in front of you.

Next, bring your knee up to waist height with the toes curled up.

Snap your leg forward and straighten your knee. Keep your toes curled up.

Bend your knee back to regain your balance before putting your foot back down on the floor.

Upper Level Block

To start a upper level block, start by standing in a ready stance with your left foot forward and your knees bent.

Next, raise your hand so that the wrist is eye level.

Lower Block

Stand in a ready stance.

Lean forward, bring the arm down and block with the wrist. The fist should be over the knee.

Side Kick

For the side kick, start by standing in a ready stance.

Next, bring your knee straight up.

Turn your hip over and kick forward with the heel. The foot should be turned and pointing to the side.

Bend your knee back to regain your balance before putting your foot back down on the floor.

If you would like helpful information about the martial arts for children, watch a video for parents, and down-
load the free e-guide "The Parents Guide To Martial Arts and
Choosing a School," join us at www.kidskarateproject.com

Check out author David B. Nemeroff's other book, *Enter into Aikido*. Visit his official website www.Aikido-Dojo.com for more information about David and/or the martial arts.

www.ingramcontent.com/pod-product-compliance
Lightning Source LLC
Chambersburg PA
CBHW042129030726
47599CB00002B/407